Headlong

'   ountry's most
€   ng touring company'
Daily Telegraph

'Headlong is one of the jewels of regional theatre'
Independent

H   g is one of the UK's leading
t   companies. Led by award-
v   Artistic Director Rupert
C   adlong is dedicated to new
v   making theatre. We
c   e   n the most exciting
a   nt   s theatre artists in the
c   nd   ovide them with the
t   sou   s and creative support
t   the   to make their most
c   enging work.

V   nterested in theatre that
a   ovocative questions of the
wo   we live in today in the most
vib   and theatrical forms we can
imagine. The focus of our work is new
writing but we also look to develop
new and emerging artists through
dynamic and ambitious revivals. We
run workshops and placement
programmes for the writers,
directors, designers and producers of
the future; practitioners who have
emerged under Headlong's support
are now some of the leading theatre
ar   around the world.

Previous work includes: *The Effect*
(National Theatre); *Medea* (UK tour);
Boys (HighTide Festival/The Nuffield,
Southampton/Soho Theatre);
Romeo and Juliet (UK tour); *Decade*
(St Katharine Docks); *Earthquakes in
London* (National Theatre/UK tour);
Enron (Chichester Festival Theatre/
Royal Court/West End/UK tour/
Broadway); *Elektra* (Young Vic);
Faustus, Salome (UK tour/Hampstead
Theatre); *Six Characters in Search
of an Author* (Chichester Festival
Theatre/West End/UK tour/Sydney/
Perth); *Edward Gant's Amazing Feats
of Loneliness* (UK tour/Soho Theatre);
King Lear (Liverpool Everyman/Young
Vic); *Three Sisters, Lulu, Medea
Medea* (The Gate); *The Last Days of
Judas Iscariot* (Almeida Theatre);
Rough Crossings, Angels in America
(UK tour/Lyric, Hammersmith);
*A Midsummer Night's Dream, The
English Game, The Winter's Tale,
Restoration, Paradise Lost* (UK tour).

Artistic Director	Rupert Goold
Executive Producer	Henny Finch
Associate Director	Robert Icke
Finance Manager	Julie Renwick
Assistant Producer	Lindsey Alvis
Assistant Producer	Stephen Daly
Production Assistant	Claire Turner
(Stage One Apprentice)	
Associate Artist	Sarah Grochala

The Nuffield southampton

Over the last forty years The Nuffield has grown from an in-house producer of new plays, and neglected classics, to a broader remit incorporating a series of exciting collaborations across new spaces and venues. Award-winning Nuffield productions and co-productions tour nationally and internationally, while the theatre also presents some of the best contemporary theatre from this country and abroad, and hosts two resident companies: Apples and Snakes South East, and Grist to the Mill (co-hosted with The Puppet Centre).

The Nuffield has become a vital artistic resource for the region, investing in developing new artists and providing a full and varied educational and participatory programme including an acclaimed two-year writers' group for talented developing playwrights, several of whom have gone on to win professional acclaim, and being home to Hampshire Youth Theatre.

On June 1st this year Patrick Sandford and Kate Anderson will step down as joint CEOs of The Nuffield. By this time the duo will have been at the helm of this exciting company for a combined total of 37 years (25 for Patrick and 12 for Kate), and they will be leaving it in great shape for Sam Hodges to take over as The Nuffield adopts a producer-led model.

Under Kate and Patrick, The Nuffield has developed a long-standing co-producing relationship with Headlong. Each spring, we work together to provide a talented, emerging director with a main stage classic production. This year we are very pleased to be working with Blanche McIntyre (*'Last year Blanche McIntyre officially became theatre's Next Big Thing,'* The Independent) on one of our favourite plays, *The Seagull*. This is our fifth co-production in this series following: *Romeo and Juliet*, *A Midsummer Night's Dream*, *The Winter's Tale*, and Edward Gant's *Amazing Feats of Loneliness*.

For more information on what's happening at The Nuffield, please visit **www.nuffieldtheatre.co.uk**, Facebook **on.fb.me/Nuffield** or Twitter**@nuffieldtheatre**.

Artistic Director Patrick Sandford
Executive Director Kate Anderson
Associate Director and Head of Creative Learning Russ Tunney
Head of Finance John Auger
Head of Production and Technical Services Julie Bisco
Head of Fundraising
Deborah Edgington
Head of Marketing - Seasonal
Sally Anne Lowe
Marketing Manager - Seasonal
Andrea Sheppard

April 2013

DERBY THEATRE

Derby Theatre has a long and rich history of delivering high quality drama to audiences. Previously Derby Playhouse, Derby Theatre, which sits at the heart of the city, is now owned and run by the University of Derby. The theatre is rooted in the local community but international in its outlook. We produce and present high quality performances working with the best local, regional and national talent.

In 2012 the theatre was awarded strategic funding by Arts Council England to develop a new model for regional theatre in the twenty-first century. From 2013, under the new artistic directorship of Sarah Brigham, we are transforming from a traditional producing house to an organisation of training, mentorship and artistic excellence; we will be an exemplar, a new way of looking at the role and responsibility of theatre to its community. Our focus will ensure that each part of our process will be open to public learning opportunities. Bringing creatives and audiences on a creative path via the co-production of narratives, rooted in local need but international in outlook, and this will build our ability to take artistic risks.

Acknowledgements

The author would like to thank the following:
Blanche McIntyre, Tim Carroll and the Factory,
Lisa Foster, Rob Icke, Henny Finch, Headlong,
and Helen Rappaport for the literal translation

@IndexCensorship

@UKuncut

@propershameful

The Seagull

Anton Chekhov, Russian dramatist and short-story writer, was born in 1860, the son of a grocer and the grandson of a serf. After graduating in medicine from Moscow University in 1884, he began to make his name in the theatre with the one-act comedies *The Bear*, *The Proposal* and *The Wedding*. His earliest full-length plays, *Ivanov* (1887) and *The Wood Demon* (1889), were not successful, and *The Seagull*, produced in 1896, was a failure until a triumphant revival by the Moscow Art Theatre in 1898. This was followed by *Uncle Vanya* (1899), *Three Sisters* (1901) and *The Cherry Orchard* (1904), shortly after the production of which Chekhov died. The first English translations of his plays were performed within five years of his death.

John Donnelly's plays include *Bone* (Royal Court Theatre), *Corporate Rock* (Nabokov/Latitude Festival), *Conversation #1* (The Factory/V&A/Latitude Festival/ SGP), *Songs of Grace and Redemption* (Liminal Theatre/ Theatre 503), *Encourage the Others* (Almeida Lab), *Burning Bird* (Synergy/Unicorn Theatre) and *The Knowledge* (Bush).

also by John Donnelly from Faber

BONE
SONGS OF GRACE AND REDEMPTION
THE KNOWLEDGE

ANTON CHEKHOV

The Seagull

a version by
JOHN DONNELLY

faber and faber

First published in 2013
by Faber and Faber Limited
74–77 Great Russell Street
London WC1B 3DA

Typeset by Country Setting, Kingsdown, Kent CT14 8ES
Printed in England by CPI Group (UK) Ltd, Croydon CR0 4YY

A CIP record for this book
is available from the British Library

978-0-571-30723-4

2 4 6 8 10 9 7 5 3 1

For Frances and Cillian

The Seagull in this version was a co-production between Headlong and The Nuffield, Southampton, in association with Derby Theatre. It was first performed at The Nuffield, Southampton, on 11 April 2013, at the start of a UK tour. The cast, in alphabetical order, was as follows:

Yevgeny David Beames
Nina Pearl Chanda
Konstantin Alexander Cobb
Irina Abigail Cruttenden
Polina Catherine Cusack
Semyon Rudi Dharmalingam
Ilya John Elkington
Yakov Eddie Eyre
Petr Colin Haigh
Masha Jenny Rainsford
Boris Gyuri Sarossy

Director Blanche McIntyre
Designer Laura Hopkins
Lighting Designer Guy Hoare
Sound Designer Gregory Clarke

Author's Notes

The play is set on the stage on which it is performed. At various times this may represent a lake by a house. Or a house by a lake.

At times, the actors address the audience directly.

Actions, pauses, and so on should be inferred from the text. Occasionally, for clarity, these are provided.

A slash mark (/) represents the point at which the following character begins to speak.

A dash (–) at the end of a line indicates that the speaker has been interrupted, either by another speaker, or a new thought of their own.

Dialogue in parentheses ( ) indicates a change in direction of thought or a switch in the person being addressed.

Songs

At various points, Petr and Yevgeny sing or hum popular songs that might be drawn – in the main, but not exclusively – from their childhood. I have chosen romantic songs tinged with sadness, regret (and not a little quiet anger in at least one instance). Future productions may well wish to use other songs felt to be more appropriate.

Characters

Yakov

Semyon

Masha

Konstantin

Petr

Nina

Yevgeny

Polina

Ilya

Irina

Boris

THE SEAGULL

A Comedy

'I can't stop them, can I?
So let them translate away;
no sense of it will come in any case.'

Anton Chekhov

One

A lake. Yakov constructs a set.
A gunshot. A flock of birds disperse.
Semyon.
Enter Masha. A rolled cigarette in her mouth.

Semyon Oh

Who died?

Masha Why, I did. Every day, always do, can't you tell?

Semyon lights her cigarette.

Semyon Know how much I earn?

Masha Yes

Semyon Two-thirty a month, that's me, my mum, two sisters, I have to take on extra students to even come close

Masha I know

Semyon The point –

Masha Not everything has to be about money

Semyon No, not unless you want to eat

Masha You can be poor and happy, it can be done –

Semyon You've read too many books

Masha Says the teacher – no one's read too many books

Semyon I have. That's my problem. Books on maths, the natural sciences – know those horseflies over there have a life cycle precisely –

Masha You think he'll be here soon?

Semyon Ah yes. Tonight by the light of the moon, the artistic souls of / Mr Treplev and Miss Zarechnaya –

Masha Artistic souls!

Semyon – will intermingle in the noblest of dramatic endeavours and become one flesh, their two souls merging in a perfect act of creation

Masha Yes

Semyon Who am I kidding? Why would you want to be with someone like me?

Masha Well, if you put it like *that*

'I burn for you. I ache for you. I'd die for you.'

With you it's all butter and taxes. Have a fag

Semyon It's not a cigarette I want. I don't even smoke

Masha So why carry a lighter?

It's closing in on us. Can feel it

My dress is sticking to my thighs

Semyon Please

Masha Sorry, that was –

Enter Konstantin and Petr.

Petr Haven't the foggiest who I am out here, all I do is sleep. In bed by ten, up at nine feeling like one of those damn birds has shat in my head, it's endless. Like one of those nightmares you wake from only to find you're still dreaming – What are those staircases, the ones that go round, begins with an 'r'?

Konstantin Escher?

Petr That's the chap

Konstantin You should move into town, bit of life'd do you good

Petr Life! That sour-faced bastard, whatever happened to him?

Konstantin Valued members of the audience, so pleased you can make the performance, but until you're called, I'd be ever so grateful if you could ah –

Semyon Bugger off?

Konstantin Exactly

Petr Masha, be a dear, ask your father to let that infernal hound off its leash, its yowling kept my sister up half the night

Masha Do it yourself, you're his boss. (*To Semyon.*) Oh come on, you

Semyon You'll let us know when – yeah

Exit Masha and Semyon.

Petr It's the respect, you see, you can't buy that

Lifetime in the civil service wishing my life away, for this – country living. Last day of work they gave me a gold watch, a card, told me to sod off. 'We'll visit.' Lying swine

Used to look forward to holidays, was what kept me going, thought of coming here. Never could wait to clear off, away from all the requisitions and stewed coffee and so on but soon as you pitch up, take one look around and . . . 'What the hell was I thinking? There's nothing to do. Except die. And drink more coffee.' I'm trapped

Yakov I'm having a swim

Konstantin We're about to start

Ten minutes

Yakov exits.

The lake. Such majesty in nature. Eight thirty-one the moon'll rise over the woods and who needs scenery?

Petr Magic

Konstantin Course if Nina's not here soon, we may as well do it in a bloody theatre. Where's she got to? Getting her out the house what with her old man and the wicked stepmother, it's like a prison break

Uncle. Couldn't you have made an effort?

Konstantin tidies Petr up.

Petr I thought I had, story of my life. First year I was in the civil service, I was outside the municipal building on a break, holding a cup of coffee, like that. Some cheeky sod popped some coins in. Hadn't even finished the coffee. Women never looked twice at me, unless it was to laugh. What the hell's up with my sister?

Konstantin A heady combination of boredom and jealousy. I made the schoolboy error of casting Nina instead of her. Not that she ever would have wanted to do it, you understand, it's not *proper* theatre. Hasn't even read it, she hates it

Petr Oh come now

Konstantin It's true – you know what Mummy's like – she's mental. I mean, brilliant, obviously. One minute she's crying over some awful train-station novel, next thing she's leapt on to the stage at a benefit for some *cause du jour* – reciting political poetry, completely uninvited – prisoners of conscience or the self-actualisation of her vagina. Once, someone collapsed in the audience, she jumped down, gave them the kiss of life, right there and then

Petr I remember

Konstantin She's more than happy to bare her soul – and the rest, if the lighting's up to scratch – all in the name of art. But try complimenting another actress. Seriously. Adopt brace position. She's the only one! No one else! She's an addict, she feeds off it, remember when she lost out on that award to She Who Mustn't Be Named?

Petr I do

Konstantin I'm not knocking her, I mean audiences adore her, but that's the problem. Out here she's no longer Arkadina, grande dame of the stage. Out here she's just . . . Irina

Petr Or your mum

Konstantin And if the stars aren't aligned, she won't lift a finger. All her money goes on charlatans and quacks, but if her only son asks for a small loan, 'I'm a working actress! I have nothing! Nothing!' I've seen her statements, she'll be all right. When the time comes, she won't be retiring on bread and water, put it that way. Where's Nina got to?

Petr It's all in your head, your mother worships you

Konstantin Let's see what the gods have to say about that. Heads she does, tails she –

He flips a coin.

Two out of three

Petr You're working yourself up over nothing.

Konstantin You're right. She doesn't love me. Why would she? She's better off without me, that way she can

17

be twenty-nine – when I'm around she has to be thirty-nine, even that's pushing it. Eternal youth, that's what she wants, 'I'm a woman, Kostya, with a woman's needs' – well exactly, how d'you think I feel?

She knows I don't respect her career. Thinks she's serving the eternal flame of high art – high arse more like. I'm sorry, the theatre is stuck. It's like this thing that's been around so long everyone's got used to it and now it's just here and no one knows why any more

Petr I know the feeling

Konstantin I can tell you what's going to happen in any given play within two minutes of it starting

Petr Ooh, I love guessing the end

Konstantin Someone comes on, they do a job – a banker or a doctor or a –

Petr – state prosecutor in the civil service

Konstantin Exactly, and their job's a metaphor for – you know, life – then they meet someone and they fall in love and grow a conscience and feel bad and finally after two hours we can all go home and pretend we liked it 'cause if we didn't we'd have to admit we wasted a fortune on getting a bad back. Then the critics praise it for its insight, when all they really mean is they agree with whatever trite moral's being peddled this week. I feel like Maupassant when he saw the Eiffel Tower and ran screaming from the vulgarity of it all

Petr He was French. Oh come on, you love it, all this. Bit of escapism, we all do

Konstantin We're sleepwalking into oblivion! We need to wake up. And it's not going to happen with the old theatre. That's why we have to tear it down

Petr And put what in its place?

Konstantin I love my mother, but everything she stands for is noise. I'd rather have nothing than live a lie

These days she's always in the papers with her *author*. His novels were one thing, but the plays –

Sometimes I wish she wasn't this *thing*, that she was just . . . Mummy. She used to throw these parties – artists, publishers, dancers, and I was the only one had no reason to be there. Torture. 'What are you working on?' – Even if I did answer, it was only a matter of time before their eyes would glaze over 'cause someone more famous than me – which was everyone – had strolled in

I mean, it's desperate, I can hear myself, I feel so stupid, but what am I, really? I'm not a writer – I'm not. I even failed at being a student, got chucked out for being part of a demonstration

Petr I thought you pissed on a statue

Konstantin It was a gesture!

Petr Couldn't you have written a letter?

Konstantin Words aren't enough, not any more. The world is changing, we're getting left behind. I need to do something, be heard, be someone

Petr You are

Konstantin Yeah, a travelling salesman's son from Kiev

Petr I saw your father act, Konstantin, and he wasn't at all bad

Konstantin Better than we thought as it turns out

Petr So come on, what's this author like then? Hardly says a word

Konstantin As far as that sort of late-thirties generation goes, I mean he's he's he's good, no, he is. Clever, straightforward, drinks craft beer. Something sad about him. Made a name for himself, anyway. Sort of stuff that wins awards. If you've read Tolstoy or Zola, you won't get much from Boris Trigorin, but he's, yeah

Petr Well, I love a literary man, always have. Once upon a time I wanted two things. The love of a good woman and my name on a book. Didn't manage either. Even a minor author, I'm not –

Konstantin Ah! It's like she's a part of me, I can feel her footsteps up through the ground in my gut

I can't live without her. Oh God, you mustn't listen to a word I say, I'm completely mad!

Enter Nina.

Release me from this curse! Release me with a kiss!

Konstantin kisses Nina.

Nina I'm not late am I, I'm not late?

Konstantin No, no, we're fine, it's all fine!

Nina I've been terrified all day, sat in my room, waiting for my father to take his wife out to their meeting, thought they'd never leave. From my window I saw the sky turning a deep red and the moon on the rise. The moment I heard that door close, I was out, and I ran and I ran and I ran and I ran and

Petr You're here now, you're here now

Nina I'm so happy!

Petr There's no need for that, you're safe! You're here with us now!

Nina Hardly speak, my lungs! Half an hour, that's it, if they knew I was here –

Konstantin We should call the others

Petr You stay, I'll fetch the troops

Petr sings the opening couplet from 'Two Little Boys' by Madden and Morse.

I once sang that at a works do. One of the junior lawyers, nice chap, said, 'Chief Prosecutor' – this was before I joined the council – 'Have you ever considered turning professional?' I said, 'No, why d'you ask?' He said, 'Well, don't, you're bloody hopeless.' Ta-ta!

Exit Petr.

Nina My father and his wife think you're all going to hell

Konstantin Maybe we are

Nina They're terrified I'll choose the theatre. I can't keep away. Drawn here. To that lake. Like a bird

Konstantin Very good

She looks at the lake.

Nina My heart is full of you

She turns to Konstantin, smiles.

Konstantin It's just us

Nina kisses Konstantin, then immediately breaks off.

Nina What's that tree?

Konstantin Elm

Nina Why is it so dark tonight?

Konstantin So the vampires feel safe. Stay

Nina I can't

Konstantin What if I came to you? By the light of the moon, when your parents are asleep? Show you my fangs

Nina The dog would bark

Konstantin I love you

Nina puts a finger to her own lips, shushes Konstantin with another.

Who's there?

Yakov?

Enter Yakov, shirtless, wet from the swim. He stares at Nina. She returns his gaze.

Frightened me half to death

It's nearly time. The moon'll be up

Are the meths and the sulphur ready?

Yakov Yes

Konstantin When we see the devil's eyes, I need them to breathe him in, to ingest him, yes?

Yakov exits.

Why are you laughing? You nervous?

Nina A little. More than a little, I'm terrified

Konstantin Don't worry about Mummy, she's –

Nina Not your mother – Boris Trigorin. Butterflies in my tummy, I feel ashamed

Konstantin Don't be

Nina It's thrilling. An actual writer, here. Is he young?

Konstantin Suppose so

Nina Don't you think he's good?

Konstantin Well, you'd think so from the interviews he gives

Nina There's no actual characters in your play, why is that?

Konstantin Actual –? This is – I'm not doing that, anyone can do that. I'm not writing how things are or how they should be, it's an invocation, ushering in a new consciousness, an entire new way of seeing the world!

Nina Some of it's difficult to say, it doesn't sit right in your mouth. Can I change some of the words?

Konstantin No!

Nina You talk about it living

Konstantin You can't just change the words

Nina Why not?

Konstantin 'Cause then it's something else

Nina What about the movements, can I change those?

Konstantin Which movements?

Nina I don't know, that's the point

Enter Yevgeny.

Your play leaves me cold, there's no love in it

Konstantin No love? What does that even mean, no love?

Exit Nina and Konstantin.
Enter Polina.

Polina Where's your wellies?

Yevgeny Don't do that!

Polina You'll catch your death

Yevgeny I'm burning up as it is

Polina You do this on purpose, trying to drive me to an early grave – well, it's working, your feet are soaked!

Yevgeny (*half sings, half hums*) 'What do you get when you fall in love?'

Polina Last night you sat out on the terrace with the grande dame herself all evening just to spite me

> *Yevgeny half sings/half hums the second verse from 'I'll Never Fall in Love Again' by Bacharach and David, a line at a time. He omits the reference to a phone, humming it rather than singing.*

Yevgeny (*half sings, half hums*)

Polina Last night you sat out on the terrace with the grande dame herself all evening just to spite me

Yevgeny (*half sings, half hums*)

Polina So wrapped up in tales of her latest theatrical exploits, didn't notice the damp

Polina You like her, don't you?

Yevgeny I'm fifty-five

Polina You need to look after your chest

It's different for men, you only get better looking as you get older, it's not fair

> *He leads her in a gentle dance.*

Yevgeny Tell me what to do

Polina What is it with men and actresses, send you all gaga, soon as you lay eyes on one, your brains go to mush?

Yevgeny (*half sings, half hums*)

If society elevates artists and treats them differently from say, plumbers or even doctors, well what's that apart from a sort of idealism?

Polina And women flinging themselves at you, that's a sort of idealism too, is it? And don't sing, I'm immune. Had all my jabs

Yevgeny Once upon a time, I was the only decent obstetrician round here

Polina And we're all ever so grateful

Yevgeny I don't recall any complaints

Polina And why do you think that was?

Yevgeny Doctor's hands. Plus I was always straight with people. Curtain up

>*They part, quickly.*
> *Enter Ilya, Irina, Petr, Boris, Semyon and Masha.*

Ilya Twenty years ago, her Ophelia at the Poltava Festival was the best I've seen

Irina Twenty years, you must be thinking of someone else

Ilya Pavel Semenych Chadin, there's another one

Irina What is he talking about, you've completely lost me!

Ilya In *Krechinsky's Wedding*, with nothing but a look, an eye patch and an ill-fitting grey suit he brought the house down. Don't make 'em like old Pavel any more

Irina Darling, these are names from another lifetime

>*Enter Konstantin.*

Ilya Where did he go, that's what I want to know? A look. Back then, mighty oaks. Now – stumps. Madam, you're a throwback to a golden age

Yevgeny There are fewer star turns these days, I'll give you that, but overall the standard's much higher

Ilya Stick to what you know, Doctor, that's my advice. In the kingdom of the one-eyed man, he who has both eyes has the last laugh over the man with one eye

Irina Kostya darling, are we starting?

Konstantin In precisely forty-six seconds, so if you would all be good enough to take your places, we'll –

Irina
'Oh Hamlet, speak no more!
Thou turns't mine eyes into my very soul;
And there I see such black and grained spots
As will not leave their tinct'

Konstantin
'You are the queen, your husband's brother's wife;
And – would it were not so! – You are my mother'

Ye ancient gods of this wood, this lake! Lead us now into the realm of dreams so we may see what will be of this earth two hundred thousand years from now!

Petr Two hundred thousand years, this'll all be razed to the ground

Konstantin Then that's what you'll see

Irina After that bloody dog of yours kept me up, a realm of dreams sounds very tempting, I must say

The Birdwoman (Nina) emerges from the lake. It has the body of a woman and the head of a giant bird. It wears a light white dress, rendered sheer by the water. It holds aloft a prism.

Birdwoman I howl into the void. And hear nothing back

All living creatures. Antelope and eagle. Hummingbird and lion. Mollusc and rat

Bone

Stone

Gone

None remains, except I –

I am Mars. I am Venus. I am Alexander. I am Joan

Man, Woman, Beast

The consciousness of every living thing

What was, what is, and is to come

Irina It's very German, isn't it?

Birdwoman I am beyond comprehension

Irina Oh come on, give us a chance

Konstantin Mummy –

Birdwoman My adversary the devil – father of eternal matter – is lonely

He wanders the void, an outcast, adrift in this quintessence of dust

Matter and spirit must become one flesh, the universal soul

Life itself must be reborn

I must bear his heir or there will be no air to breathe for all eternity. See!

His crimson eyes – his essence!

I offer myself. A virgin sacrifice to fill this earth anew

I fuck the devil

I fuck the devil

Nina writhes and groans.

Horror! Horror!

A quiver of life

My cunt is angry

Irina Furious, one imagines

Birdwoman Something moves inside me

I feel you growing in my belly

I part my lips to speak

    Nina births a child.

Irina Is that an eggy smell?

Konstantin Sulphur

Irina It's an effect

Konstantin Please

Birdwoman A new dawn. But wait!

The devil devours his child!

Polina (*to Yevgeny*) Your hat, you'll catch cold

Irina Well, I was taught it's good manners to take one's hat off when someone's eating, especially when the lord of eternal matter's popped in for tea

Konstantin All right, show's over, that's it

Irina We're in the middle of the play, you can't just –

Konstantin I said show's over

    Exit Nina.

I apologise, the the the the nerve of even contemplating –

Irina Oh come on

Konstantin – to violate the sanctity, the monopoly, the chosen few, the – amateurs!

    Exit Konstantin.

Irina What was that about?

Petr Irina, for goodness –

Irina No – no – will someone please tell me what –

Petr He's a young man

Irina He said it was a bit of fun and that's how I approached it

Petr You offended him

Irina No one told me I was watching a masterpiece, I know exactly what he was up to, he was teaching us a lesson on the true meaning of theatre, it was a wilful attack. He's a self-centred petulant little boy and he needs to bloody well grow up

Petr He wants your approval

Irina He's a funny way of going about it – you're going to stink the place out like a skunk's fart and do ghastly things with the master of eternal matter, you deserve all you get. He might think he's ushering in a new era, all I see is a load of gimmicky outré tosh

Boris You can only write the next play

Irina Well, that's fine but no one has to watch it, do they? It's indulgent and it makes me cross. I've seen this sort of thing before and all it sets out to do is provoke –

Yevgeny And did he succeed?

Irina I'm not angry actually, so much as bored, and that's the worst crime of all. I certainly didn't mean to offend his whatever

Semyon You know they found the part of the brain where the soul lives? Scientists

Someone should write a play about a teacher. Something meaty. There's things that go on behind –

Irina I think we're going to leave meat and sections of the brain for the time being, don't you?

Look at it, what a beautiful evening!

Is that singing? D'you hear?

Polina Across the lake

Irina beckons Boris near, takes his hand.

Irina Oh, how enchanting. There used to be six country houses on this side of the lake, all in a line – parties, gunshots, laughter!

Ilya fires his gun into the air. They jump and then laugh.

And the affairs, God, like a carousel – this was ten, fifteen years ago, mind, so I must have been – *don't you say a word*! And the leading man in all this carry on, the Idol of the Six Estates – none other than Doctor Yevgeny Dorn. Dorn Juan we called him. Still debonair of course but then – his famous bedside manner . . .

Yevgeny gives the same gesture that accompanied his earlier 'doctor's hands' remark.

I'm having a pang. I was awful to my baby, simply vile. God, do you think he'll forgive me?

Enter Nina, a blanket around her.

Masha I'll go

Irina Would you?

Masha Konstantin! Konstantin!

Exit Masha, calling.

Nina I think that might be it as far as the show goes

Petr Encore! Encore!

Irina 'Bravo', I think, Petr! Such a bold performance, your whole look and your voice, the – Cover up, you'll catch your death! How talented is this one? Seething with envy! You're wasted on this lot, I order you on to the stage this minute, go!

Nina I dream of it. I just can't imagine it ever happening

Irina One never can. Have you met Boris Trigorin, by the way? I think you've got a fan

Nina I know who you are. I've read everything . . .

Irina Gosh, that is a lot. Don't be shy. Once you get past all the brilliance, he's deeply ordinary. Oh look, he's being bashful

Yevgeny Might want to clear some of this . . . Gives me the willies

Ilya Yakov

Yakov clears the performance debris.

Nina It's a strange play, isn't it?

Boris Well, I can't say I understood much, but you were very good. Honest (*as in 'truthful'*). And it looked amazing

Are there fish? In the lake, I mean

Nina Yes

Boris Fish are honest. I love sitting on the bank as the light . . . watching the float for the . . . merest . . .

Nina I always imagined when you know what it is to create something all other pleasure is just a distraction

Irina Careful, he's like the fish, he scares easily

Ilya I saw Silva give his Othello once, you know, Verdi. Moscow Opera. Magnificent. He was blacked up so pretty sure it was Othello. Couldn't get away with it these days. Anyway, Silva hits his famous lower C – exactly! But get this – the bass from our church choir, he's sat in the cheap seats, up in the gods – and just as Silva hits his lower C, from above us . . . 'Bravo Silva!' An entire octave lower. Imagine that. Could have heard a pin drop

Yevgeny Someone just walked over my grave

Nina I have to go

Irina So soon?

Nina I'm sorry

Irina We were hoping you could stay!

Nina It's my father, I –

Irina Oh that man, I'm not even going to go there

Well look, you must come back

Nina I don't want to leave

Irina Now, someone should make sure she gets home safe

Nina No, please

Petr Don't be silly, one hour, what's the harm?

Nina Thank you, Petr, I mean it, thank you

Sorry

   Exit Nina.

Petr Ridiculous

Irina You know her mother left all the money to the father. Now he's shacked up with some awful bloody woman and cut that poor girl out the will entirely. I could scream

Yevgeny He's a fucking pig, her old man – I'm sorry, but he is

Petr It's the joints I'm afraid, I need to be heading in

Irina His knees, they're made of rotten old wood, come on, Hopalong, let's plonk you by the fire

Petr Hear that bloody hound again, what's it guarding, the gates of hell?

Ilya The lower barn

Petr Mr Shamraev, will you please let it off its leash, give us all some respite?

Ilya If that grain goes, you'll be pulling the carriages yourself all winter, so in a word, no

Petr Well put it out of its misery somehow

Ilya 'Bravo Silva!' A bass from a church choir, imagine!

Semyon D'you get paid for running a choir?

All exit, except for Yevgeny and Polina, who linger, as does Ilya.

Ilya Madam

Exit Polina and Ilya.
Yevgeny is alone.

Yevgeny Well, maybe it's my age, but I liked it – the play. And that girl, when she talked about wandering the earth alone, the red eyes of the devil – I don't know about you, I was shaking like a leaf. Sure it was . . . and the bit with the . . . but it had something, it was . . . fresh

He's coming back on in a sec and I'm going to say something nice

Enter Konstantin.

Konstantin Gone

Yevgeny I'm here

Konstantin I'm trying to evade Masha's clutches, hear her yelping my name

Yevgeny Konstantin Treplev, I loved your play. Yes, it was mad as a horse and we missed the end –

Konstantin The prism was supposed to refract the moonlight!

Yevgeny – it did something to me, and that's rare. You're on to something

Konstantin embraces Yevgeny.

Oh, tears! Okay, okay. Now, you've got this terrific abstract imagination and it's bursting with ideas which in my book is exactly what art should be, but it needs . . . All the blood's gone from your face, are you all right?

Konstantin I should carry on?

Yevgeny Yes, but only show what matters, what lasts, how do I put this – I've lived. Done rather a lot of living, in fact, more than most – all creeds and colours

Konstantin Sorry, is this –

Yevgeny What I'm saying is if I could forgo everything I've done for one moment of artistic –

Konstantin I was actually looking for Nina

Yevgeny You need to know what you're trying to achieve, but also *why* – if you set off on this path without a clear focus, it will ruin you, I've seen it, it will swallow you whole

Konstantin Have you seen her or not?

Yevgeny Who?

Konstantin Nina

Yevgeny She's gone home

Konstantin What do you mean, she can't have gone, why didn't you say?

Yevgeny My dear boy, get a hold of yourself

Konstantin Thanks but if it's all the same –

Enter Masha.

34

Masha Your mother's worried about you

Konstantin Tell her I'm not here. And please! You're like
a dog –

Yevgeny Now hang on

Konstantin Yapping around

Yevgeny That's not on

Konstantin Doctor, thank you, I mean that, but –

Exit Konstantin.

Yevgeny What is it with this generation?

*Masha pops a cigarette in her mouth, searches for a
lighter.*

Masha You know someone's run out of things to say
when they start complaining about 'this generation'

*Yevgeny snatches the cigarette from Masha's mouth
and tosses it.*

Yevgeny Filthy bloody habit – poison

They're playing cards, I said I'd make up numbers

Masha Wait, I

My father he – I can't – the thing is, we don't connect
and

I always felt I could talk to you –

*Masha is very close to Yevgeny. They are close enough
to kiss. They don't.*

What am I doing?

I'm scared I might do something

Yevgeny What do you mean?

Masha I need this pain to stop. I've never said these words out loud before. I'm in love

I am, I'm in love with Konstantin, I love him

Yevgeny Come here

Mad as each other, the lot of you

Must be something in the water, all this love

I'm telling you, it's that bloody lake

Two

The Sun. Heat.
  Irina, Yevgeny, Masha. Yevgeny reads silently.

Irina Come on. Up, up. Up you get

You are twenty and I'm . . . nearly twice that. Doctor
Dorn, which of us looks younger?

Yevgeny Always you, darling

Irina And why d'you think that is? I'll tell you. I keep
myself physically and mentally agile. You – you just
vegetate. Sweetie, I'm only saying what everyone thinks.
You're all – (*Groans, miming the air going out.*) Life!

Golden rule, always live in the here and now, plan ahead
too much you get nothing done, you get the glooms.
We're all going to die! Well of course we're going to die,
there's no point harping on about it

Masha I was born in the wrong century

Irina I know the feeling, it's so backwards here

Masha I mean I was born too late, always two steps
behind. What's the point? God, I'm depressing myself

Irina Mmm

Masha Need to snap out of it

Irina What you need is a makeover

  *Yevgeny hums a line from 'I'll Never Fall in Love
  Again' by Johnnie Ray.*

Irina Attention to detail, it's how I keep my looks.

Otherwise . . . (*She blows imaginary dust from her palm.*)
Passes you by . . . hair just so, *comme il faut, à la mode*!
You never know who's watching, do you see, it's why I'm
always *on*? And why disappoint, people expect it?

Look at that, strong and delicate, like a gay little bird. I
could play a girl of fifteen

> *Yevgeny mouths 'Five–O' to Masha. Irina casts him a
> look: 'I saw that.'*

Yevgeny Be that as it may, the merchant and the rats . . .

Irina Ah yes, the rats! Read on! Actually don't, give it
here, it's my turn

Yes, I know where we are . . . where are we, ah! 'And it
stands to reason . . . And it stands to reason' – quiet at
the back– 'that to invite a writer into your home by way
of flattery and fine words is as dangerous as a corn
merchant keeping rats in his barns (?!). And yet we love
them. So when a woman has set her sights on a writer
(!!), she lays siege to him with compliments and any
favour you care to imagine' – well that's written by a
man! The French might go in for that sort of thing but
we are a civilised people. Over here we at least do these
poor men the courtesy of falling head over heels before
we pounce! First time I saw Boris I didn't know if I was
going or coming

> *Enter Petr – with a walking stick. Semyon pushes a
> wheelchair. Also Nina.*

Petr And aren't we a happy girl? All sweetness and light!

Look who we found! Daddy and Stepmummy are out of
town so it's three whole days of fun and games!

Nina (*to Irina*) Nina Zarechnaya, at your disposal

Petr Isn't she just – I could eat her up!

Irina Yes. Clever little thing, aren't you? But too much praise brings bad luck, and we don't want that – Now has anyone seen my Boris?

Nina He's fishing

Irina Is he?

Nina At the bathing place

Irina It's a wonder he finds so much to do there

Nina What are you reading?

Irina (*brushing her off*) (Maupassant, darling)
I've one of those feelings, you know when you just, in your . . . What is the matter with my son? Floats around like he's only half there and his moods – spends half his time on that bloody lake, hardly see him

Masha He's in pain. Deep in his soul

Would you do a bit from one of his plays?

Nina I just find them a little bit Germanic

Masha When he reads, he goes pale as a ghost, except his eyes, they burn. His voice is like the night air

Yevgeny Oop –

Yevgeny gestures that Petr is asleep.

Ni-night, sweet prince

Petr farts loudly.

Irina (*sing-song*) Petrusha!

Petr Yes

Irina Think we lost you for a moment there, darling

Petr I'm wide awake

Irina Are you taking your pills?

Petr What pills? This charlatan won't give me any!

Yevgeny At your age

Petr At my age? I'm your age – give or take

Yevgeny Watch yourself or I'll give you something that will shut you up

Petr Did you hear that?

Irina Isn't there somewhere we can send him, some sort of, what's the word – clinic?

Petr Clinic!

Irina No, a centre

Petr She's trying to pack me off to a home!

Irina Not a centre, a retreat, that's what I mean

Yevgeny Do it or don't, it's up to you

Irina I'm asking your opinion

Yevgeny Well it's six of one, half a dozen of the other

Irina Oh, Buddha has spoken

Petr I am here, you know

Yevgeny I'm being perfectly clear

Semyon He should give up smoking

Petr Well bollocks to you, Judas

Yevgeny Not bollocks actually, good advice

Petr One, I've only got the one vice, I'm not giving that up; two – I'm not the bloody dog, you know, I can hear you

Yevgeny Booze and fags strip you of your personality. Couple of cigars, few snifters of vodka – (*to Irina*) *or*

worse, you lose yourself. Everyone's the life and soul after a few drinks, in their own head. You're not careful you'll end up like one of those celebrities refers to himself in the third person. Petr Sorin is hungry, Petr Sorin wants a nap

Petr All right, all right, you swine, you've made your point. But you've lived! What have I done? Twenty-eight years in the civil service, and what have I got to show for it?

Yevgeny A very nice gold watch

Petr It's not funny, you've had your share of . . . frivolity, you've got . . . memories . . . and you know what, it's made you complacent, it *has*. And that's why now you're all . . . Whereas I just want to drink sherry and smoke. To forget. Because there's nothing to remember. And so on

Yevgeny You're right, it's not funny, but in your – I mean at your age – and I know, I know but to complain you didn't grab life when you had the chance – well, I'm sorry, that really is frivolous

Masha My leg's gone to sleep

Exit Masha.

Yevgeny There you go. She's got bottles hidden all over

Petr She's unhappy

Yevgeny With respect, that is unutterable horseshit

Petr You argue like someone who's forgotten why

Yevgeny Why what?

Petr Why anything

Irina Oh what could be more divine than country living? I do love you all so. There's an art to tedium, it's not as easy as it looks. The quiet. Heat. Bugger all to do except philosophise – heaven and earth, Horatio, heaven and earth. Nowt more pleasant. Except, my darling friends, being on your tod in a hotel room going over one's lines. Bliss

Nina Oh, I know, that's so true!

Petr So much better in town. Sat in your study. Secretary, so no one pitches up uninvited. Phones ringing. Cabbies who actually know where they're going . . .

Yevgeny hums the same refrain as earlier from 'I'll Never Fall in Love Again' by Johnnie Ray.
Enter Ilya and Polina.

Ilya The gang's all here! Fantastic, good morning, wonderful, health

My wife tells me you're off into town together?

Irina That's right

Ilya Wonderful, later today?

Irina Yes

Ilya No, why not? How you getting there?

Irina How am I – the carriage? I –

Ilya And which horses are you . . .?

Irina Whichever horses you normally . . .

Ilya Well, there's the horses we're using to move the rye. Are those the horses –

Irina What's he talking to me about horses for? I don't know about horses!

Ilya Fine, I'll shut down the estate for the day so you can get into town

Petr What do you mean shut down, who said anything about shut down!

Ilya Who's going to pull the carriage, muggins?

Petr The carriage horses

Ilya Oh, the carriage horses

Petr Yes

Irina I don't –

Ilya And what about harnesses?

Petr What about harnesses?

Ilya There aren't any

Petr There aren't any harnesses?

Ilya We have no harnesses! Of harnesses, we have none!

Irina Look, I don't give two hoots how, I just have to / be in town

Ilya Madam, when it comes to the theatre, I bow down before you, I –

Irina What's this –

Ilya – worship at your feet, you can have ten years of my blood, sweat and tears –

Irina What's this got to do / with anything?

Ilya – but when it comes to farming, and I mean this with the greatest respect, you haven't the first fucking clue what you're on about!

Irina I am going to Moscow and I am not coming back

Petr Oh God

Irina I will not stay in this place another second with this man, get me some horses from the village or I will put the bit between my own teeth and pull the fucking carriage myself!

Ilya That's it! I quit! Find yourself another bloody slave!

Exit Ilya.

Irina Every summer that man talks to me like this and you do nothing! I will *never* set foot in this place again

Exit Irina.
A brief moment, then:

Petr Bring me every fucking horse on this estate *this instant*!

Nina What's the matter with him? This is Irina Arkadina, not some . . . you can't talk to an artist like that! If she needs something, to hell with the estate!

Polina What do you want me to do?

Petr Look, we'll, we'll, we'll talk to her, we'll say something, anything. We'll all just calm ourselves and talk like rational and reasonable adults to that jumped up pig-headed BASTARD INGRATE! – Sorry, sorry, sorry

Nina No, no, no, sit down, sit down, this isn't good for you, we'll take you up to the house. It's dreadful, it really is

Nina and Semyon push Petr out.
Polina and Yevgeny remain.

Yevgeny So boring, aren't we? So predictable

Should've been out on his ear years ago, he's bloody lucky that husband of yours. Irina and the old man'll end up grovelling for him to stay, you watch

Polina Every day, something like this, it's so fragile. Soon as he heard our plans he sent the carriage horses out to the fields with the carthorses, if you knew how this makes me feel – I've got tremors. Look. I can't go on, Yevgeny – lover – we're not getting any younger

44

Yevgeny I'm fifty-five

It's too late to just –

Polina I know there are other women, I'm not stupid.
But you can't live with them all. There's so little time left.
Maybe if we could – consider. I'm just asking for . . .

Nina enters. She has flowers.

. . . a morsel. I'm sorry, I get jealous is all. You're a
doctor, it comes with the territory, I –

Polina gestures: 'Doctor's hands'.

Yevgeny Hello

Nina Irina's crying, Petr's having an asthma attack

Yevgeny Best give them some of my special medicine

Nina Here

Nina hands Yevgeny the flowers.

Yevgeny *Très gentil*

Yevgeny leaves – Polina follows.

Polina They're beautiful. May I?

*Yevgeny hands Polina the flowers. She rips them up
and exits, followed by Dorn.*
Nina is alone.

Nina A great actress. Crying. Over that!

Have you ever called a famous person by their own
name, to their face, I mean? It's really weird. You don't
expect them to answer

Boris Trigorin. Boris. Trigorin

In his interviews he sounds so clever, but he sweats.
When he drinks, if you sit close enough, you can smell
the beer on his breath. He gets happy when he catches

a fish, not even a big one, just an ordinary fish! His work is translated all over the world. Can you imagine? I'd love that

I used to think people like him and Irina Arkadina were aliens. I thought they hated people like us, you know, ordinary people – civilians. Their fame was a kind of revenge on society. But here they are. Fighting and fishing and . . . fooling around, like anyone. It all seemed so out of reach, but now –

Enter Konstantin carrying a gun and a dead bird – a tern.

Konstantin Who are you talking to?

Nina What's that supposed to be?

Konstantin It's an offering

Nina Looks like a dead bird to me

Konstantin I killed this seagull. And now I lay it before you

Nina I don't want it

Konstantin You know why? Because all beauty must die

Nina You even talk like your plays now

Konstantin Soon, I'll kill myself in the same way

Nina I don't know who you are

Konstantin That's 'cause you chop and change so much you don't know yourself any more – 'Frailty, thy name is woman' –

Nina Stop quoting things. Be normal

Konstantin Normal?

Nina Offerings, all this . . . Konstantin, you've just given me a dead seagull

Konstantin You ashamed of me?

Nina I'm obviously too stupid to get what you're –

Konstantin It's 'cause my play failed. That's when you started acting like this

Nina Like what?

Konstantin Cold. Feel you recede. Wouldn't believe it if I couldn't see it with my own eyes

You'll be pleased to know I burnt it, watched every last scrap go up, turn to ash and float down like autumn leaves. Funnily enough, I think it might be my best work – the pyre, I mean. Not the play, God

Nina I don't understand

Konstantin You'll forgive anything but failure, won't you, you're all the same?

Nothing but contempt – all we stood for

Think I'm just like the rest, don't you?

Nina Maybe that's not such a bad thing. Being like everyone else, for you

Konstantin Thought you were my friend. I thought you –

You're like a rat in my skull, gnawing at my brain, sucking out every last ounce of –

Boris enters with a notebook.

Bang on cue. The light of the earth. 'Words, words, words' – fucking Hamlet with a notebook.

You're melting. Well, go on then. Let the sun's rays penetrate your heart

I won't stand in your way. I see I'm casting a shadow

Exit Konstantin.
Boris jots something in his notebook.

47

Boris Roll-ups. Vodka. Black. Love. Misery

Nina Hello, Boris Trigorin

Boris Oh hello, didn't see you there

We're going. Didn't see that coming. Don't often get the chance to meet young women, well – interesting ones – and . . . when I was younger, I – I wasn't very – anyway – that was then

I'm not sure I do young women very well. Shame we didn't get to – you know – talk

I'd love to be in that head of yours, get the lie of the land so to speak

Nina I'd love to be in that head of yours

Boris Really, why?

Nina To see how it feels

Boris What feels?

Nina Fame. Success

Boris Never really thought about it. Either I'm not as famous as you think or it doesn't feel like anything

Nina But when you see your own name in the papers?

Boris Yeah, funny one that. They say something nice it's all right. But when you get a bad one – sort of hollow feeling, 'cause of course everyone knows, then after a day or two . . .

Boris gestures that it dissipates into the ether.

Nina You've no idea – I'm so jealous! Most people spend their whole lives dreaming of a – something to alleviate the pain of all this beige. No one's happy, you must have noticed, but you – this thing, this gift has landed in your lap. Come on, some days you must look in the mirror and think, you know what, I'm bloody good

Boris I think you mean well, okay, you're very young and –

Nina Your life is amazing!

Boris Look, I've got writing to be doing, I can't just stand here and – you're doing my head in, you know, I'm actually a little riled up

Exit Boris.
Re-enter Boris.

Okay, let's do this, let's talk about the magic of being me. You know how a madman will howl at the moon all night, well that's what it's like, day in, day out, 'I haven't written, I haven't written, I've got to write, I haven't written,' and without warning – it's got you. In its teeth, and as soon as this one's done, another tears you from its jaws, and on, and on, tossed from the snarling maw of one story to the next, unrelenting, without mercy, so tell me 'cause I'm missing it, does that sound like fun?

That cloud. Like a grand piano – 'cloud like a grand piano floats by'. Summer's day – bang. Those, those heliotropes, I'll pinch their sickly, sweet smell to evoke the beauty and decay of a late summer evening or I'm at the riverside with a rod and a beer – a moment's respite, then! Snaggled among the reeds, an idea! – and it's bye-bye fishing weekend. Even when I'm watching a play, there's no let up, I zone out, guppy like, start thinking a story of my own

Or or or even this. You think this is me? No, there's a fraction of me here, but most of me is out there, looking on at this whole scenario thinking, hmm, pretty girl, white dress, what does this mean? Continually gathering the pollen from my best flowers, picking them and stamping on the roots, all to ensure my audience is sated – it's not funny! Like a snake consuming its own tail, my life has no purpose other than providing fodder for my work – I can't get away from myself. Don't think you're safe – I think you'll make a nice opening to one of my stories, I'll cut your throat soon as look at you, I mean it

This is how it is! And when, and when people find out what I do: 'So what's next?' – they say that, with a fixed grin as if under strict instructions from the local madhouse to keep me talking till the men in the white coats come and cart me away; or 'What's in the pipeline?' Like it's oil, or bilge, an endless supply of this strange viscous commodity, but there's not. You've got to feed it, this thing – bits of brain, shards of bone, sinew, muscle, cannibalise those you hold most dear 'cause if you don't, you're next

You think *this* is crazy, should have seen me when I was younger – there's this gruesome stage when someone's spotted your potential and producers and publishers start inviting you to openings and launches. You don't know anyone, haven't a clue who to talk to, everyone looks so confident like they belong while you stand there clutching a glass of warm white wine like a fucking life-raft, hoping to God you're not emanating the same waves of desperation as the rest of them, but you are

And when something's actually on, the reason you supposedly do it all in the first place – agony! 'Cause you're not going to be watching your own play, God no! You're watching the audience, the critics. Why did she scratch her ear? What does that mean? She hates it! She's famous for scratching her ear, we're sunk!

Nina Okay, okay, okay, forget the rest, the instant of creation, that moment when you actually . . . surely that must make it all worthwhile?

Boris It's all right. Fleeting glimpses of something bigger, that's fine, I can cope with that. And it's nice when you get the proofs, all . . . proper. But soon as it's out there – 'It's good, but I preferred his last one.' Or 'an interesting take but not as good as Turgenev.' They'll put that on my grave. 'Here lies Boris Trigorin. He was good. But not as good as Turgenev' (the shit)

Nina Listen to yourself. You're so complacent, you've been spoiled by success

Boris What success?

Nina Oh come on

Boris I don't even like my own writing, I'm serious! Okay, this water here, the lake, these trees, the sky. Nature, portraits, yes, some irresistible urge, yes I can do that, people I'm fine with, but –

There's an obligation. Everyone wants the latest thing, the great State of the Nation novel. 'Where are all the plays about politics?' Fuck off. Trying to capture the spirit of the age, chasing shadows, trying to get hold of something which by its nature has moved on, like watching the doors close on a train for which you're perpetually late. I just don't know if I have anything to say about the world. Whenever I try and *engage* – it's all so false. You know?

Having said all that, I am bloody good at describing landscapes

Nina You have no idea how good you are. How important! How brilliant!

God, to be you, I'd give up everything like a shot. To do what you do. Inspire people, real, ordinary people and they'd look at me and say, You! You're the one! You're who we've been waiting for!'

Society needs people like us, it needs artists, the people are hungry for / truth, for joy, for hope –

Boris (The people!)

Nina (It's true!) And in return, they'll raise us up, draw us through the streets on a chariot burnished with gold!

Boris A chariot? Like in an opera with a spear and pigtails and a tin hat?

Nina I'd give anything to be an actress or a writer. Be poor, hungry – live in a bedsit, share mouldy bread with my friends the rats. The insecurity, the fear – my family would disown me, I'd take it all in my stride, gladly, all I'd ask is that people know my name. Proclaim it from the rooftops, in the streets. Nina Zarechnaya!

Dizzy just the thought!

    Irina's voice from off: 'Boris!'

Boris I really don't feel like leaving

Nina Do you see the house and garden on the other side of the lake?

It's my late mother's. I've lived here my whole life. I used to hide there. I know it all – every crevice, every fold

Boris What a wonderful thought

What's that?

Nina It's an offering

Boris Is it? Sure it's not a dead bird?

Nina Konstantin killed it. It's a seagull

Boris It's a tern, I think. The common kind. *Sterna hirundo.* Suppose that's a seagull of sorts

I really don't want to leave, maybe we could concoct something?

Why don't you have a chat with Irina? See if you can twist her arm?

Nina What are you writing?

Boris Idea for a story. A beautiful young girl lives by a lake all her life. She loves this lake. She's happy and free, like that bird was once. Then a man comes along and for no reason at all – what do you think he does?

Nina He destroys her

Boris Yes, I think so

Enter Irina.

Irina I've been looking all over

Boris I was just –

Irina We're staying

Exit Irina.
Exit Boris.
Nina is alone.

Nina This isn't real. It's a dream

Three

Luggage.
   Throughout the act Yakov shifts luggage on to the stage. Once he has finished, he shifts it all off to the other side.
   Masha and Boris.
   They both drink. Boris eats

Masha You're a writer, you can do something with that. If he'd hurt himself, I mean if he'd – you know – well, I wouldn't be here with you now, do you understand? And don't think I'm scared 'cause I'm not – courage is the one thing I'm not short of. Anyway, this love's got to go, got to rip it out

Boris How do you intend to do that?

Masha By marrying Semyon

Boris What, the teacher?

Masha Why not?

Boris Bit much

Masha Well, I need something to distract me from the endless misery of the human condition

Boris Well, it's a fair point

Masha Love without hope is agony. Least with Semyon, love'll be the last thing on my mind. It's what you do isn't it when something makes you miserable? Find something else to make you even more miserable. I don't know, kill some time, won't it? Top up?

   Boris looks at his watch.

Boris Really?

Masha Oh come off it.

Masha pours drinks as she speaks.

Can't be the first woman you've met who likes a little drink before lunch, I know we're supposed to pretend not to but we all do, the smart ones anyway. I'm just a bit more upfront. Vodka or gin with us girls, the clear ones (bottoms up)

They both drink. Masha pours again.

Just a bit of a bloke really, aren't you? Uncomplicated. I'm sorry you're off

Boris Me too

Masha Tell her you're staying

Boris Irina? No chance. Not with her son acting up. First he tries to shoot himself. And misses. Now he wants me to have a duel! I mean, come on – *really*? Sulks and snorts and skulks about the place, I don't mind him muttering about me all the time, I just wish he'd be quieter about it. Scares off all the fish

All this 'new forms' business, tear down the old guard – there is no old guard. There's plenty of room, he just can't see it

Masha He's jealous

Enter Nina.

And that really is none of my business

Masha rises.

My teacher isn't the sharpest but he's kind. And poor. And he loves me. Feel sorry for him actually – and his old mum – which I s'pose is better than complete indifference

So. New beginnings. I enjoyed our chats. Send us one of your books – write me a message in the cover – not something shit – 'Regards.' 'To Masha. Who doesn't know where she came from, where she's going, or why she's here.' Don't forget now

Masha drains her glass if she hasn't already, and exits.
Nina holds out her fists.
Boris taps one. Nina opens it. Empty. She opens the other to reveal a medallion.

Nina Trying to work out if I should be an actress or not. I was hoping for some advice

Boris It's not the sort of thing you can give advice about

Nina Take this in remembrance of me

Boris takes it.

Your initials and a line reference

Boris Page one-two-one, lines twelve and thirteen

Nina *Days and Nights* – it's my favourite of yours

I didn't know if we'll see each other again

Boris I'm charmed. Thank you

Boris kisses the medallion.

Nina Remember me

Boris As you were that day. You wore that white cotton dress. Sun was behind you. We talked. That seagull

Nina *Sterna hirundo.* Common tern

I need to see you before you go

Enter Irina and Petr. Yakov continues to carry luggage on and off.

Exit Nina.

Irina You need rest. You shouldn't be going out in your state, it's ridiculous. Air's so thick, I can feel a migraine coming on. Who was that, Nina?

Boris What? – Yes

Irina Not interrupting, I hope

This packing is exhausting

Yakov holds Boris' rods.

Yakov You want these?

Boris Yes. Keep the books. Or sell them, up to you

Yakov continues with the luggage.

One-two-one, twelve and – have you got any of my plays?

Irina Try the library

Exit Boris.

You'll make yourself ill

Petr It'll be quiet without you here

Irina What do you have to go into town for anyway?

Petr They're laying the foundation stone for the new civic hall

Irina I don't know what was wrong with the old one

Petr Some cake and bunting might do me good. Sat on my backside too long, feel like a packet of fags that's been through the laundry. I told you-know-who straight, bring the horses round for one, no mucking about. They can drop you and Boris at the station on the way.

Irina Try not to get bored while I'm gone. Or die. And

keep an eye on my son, he needs – why did he shoot himself? I'm sorry, but that's not normal. It's jealousy, I know, and the sooner I take Boris away from here the better

Petr It wasn't just that, Irina, he needs stimulation! He's a bright young man with his life ahead of him and he's stuck out here in the middle of nowhere, no job, no money, no prospects. There's nothing to do! He's ashamed. And scared. I'm fond of him – and he's fond of me – but out here he's a spare prick at a wedding and he knows it. You must see it's damaging to his pride

Irina Is there something you can do – ask one of your old pals at this stone-laying thing, see if something comes up at the town hall?

Petr Or you could give him some money – Wait, listen, he can't afford a place of his own

Irina Neither could I at his age

Petr It's different now. He's had the same coat for three years. He's a young man. It wouldn't do any harm for him to get out, see the world, do a bit of living, you know, spread his wings?

Irina For God's sake

Petr It doesn't cost as much as you think

Irina All right, I might be able to stretch to a coat, but as for 'living', it's out the question. I can't even manage the coat, I don't have any money – I don't!

Petr If you – don't get all – I'm just – I believe you! You're a generous, kind . . .

    Petr starts to laugh.

Irina I have no money!

Petr If I had money, I'd give it to him – but I don't, not a sausage. That fascist who manages my estate bleeds me dry, my entire pension pissed away on cows and bees. The bees are no good, the cows just seem to drop dead, only last week one keeled over in a ditch and there's never any bloody horses when I want them

Irina I have some money, but I'm a working actress, it's my job, there are certain practical – My wardrobe alone has nearly ruined me

Petr You're kind and I respect you and I – I – I – It's my head, I'm having one of my – sorry –

Petr collapses.

Irina Petrusha! Petrusha! Oh no, help! Someone! Fire! Fire!

Konstantin appears, head bandaged, with Semyon. Yakov enters and exits.

Something's wrong!

Petr Now don't make a fuss

Yakov returns with water.

Konstantin It's all right, Mummy, he does this, it's okay

Drink this. There you go. There you go

Petr I just need to catch my breath

I need to be in town – I'm fine! Just need a few . . .

Semyon and Yakov help Petr up and out.

Semyon Now. What's on all-fours in the morning, two feet in the afternoon, three in the evening –

Petr Yes, and at night, face down in a puddle of sherry, I can do without the school assembly

Semyon If you're well enough to talk, you're well enough to walk

Exit Petr, Semyon and Yakov.

Konstantin It's not good for him out here. He's depressed. If you could find it in your heart to give him a small loan, nothing – just a few grand, he could live in town all year round

Irina I have no money! I'm an actress, not a banker

Konstantin Please, Mummy. Will you – no one does it like you

Irina Where's a doctor when you need one?

Konstantin It's already twelve, he was supposed to be here two hours ago

Irina Sit

Irina changes Konstantin's bandage.

What do you look like? Only yesterday, a local homeless appeared at the back door asking who was our new Indian

Konstantin Mummy

Irina Barely a graze

We surmise from Irina's expression it is not barely a graze.

Now. No more shooty-shooty when Mummy's gone, okay?

Konstantin Didn't know who I was. The old black dog pitched up. Won't happen again

Konstantin kisses Irina's hands.

Healing hands. I remember when you were touring the regions – I was only small, there was a fight in the communal hall, one of the cleaners got a proper going over, kicked unconscious right in front of me, you remember? You looked after her kids while she was in hospital. You must remember?

What about those two ballet dancers who shared the flat above us, Ivan and Alexei?

Irina Ivan and Alexei! Now them I do remember!

Konstantin They used to keep us up at night, praying

Irina Ye–es

Konstantin These last few days, I've felt closer to you than I have since I was a child. I love you so much. Which is why I fail to understand what hold this man has on you

Irina He's brave and he's brilliant and it's not a hold

Konstantin Brave! That's why when I challenged him to a duel he practically shat himself and announced he was leaving that very day

Irina Darling

Konstantin He's a coward

Irina If you must know, I asked him to leave! Now you're a bright boy and I love you but I must ask you to be grown-up about this and accept the fact –

Konstantin This is exactly what he does! Look at us, arguing because of that charlatan, while all the while he's down the lake with Nina, massaging the recesses of her brain, impressing upon her the immensity of his talent

Irina Do you enjoy saying these things? I respect that man and I'll ask you one last time not to speak about him like that in my presence

Konstantin I know you want me to bow down and worship at the altar of Trigorin, like the rest of the sheep, but I don't respect him. Frankly his writing makes me want to rinse my brain out with warm piss just to get rid of the stench of –

Irina Oh, I see. You're jealous. Then that's your style, isn't it? So much easier to run real talent down, especially when you know full well you can't raise yourself to his level?

Konstantin Real talent!

Irina Well, if that's what gets you through the day –

Konstantin I've more talent in my fucking . . . knee than the rest of you have in your entire bodies!

Konstantin rips his bandage off.

You just don't see it do you? It's a landgrab! It's not enough that your lot has all the –

Irina My lot?

Konstantin – money and the power –

Irina Who the hell is my lot?

Konstantin – you need to brainwash us as well –

Irina Brain—?

Konstantin – this conspiracy of mediocrity opening your cosy plays to ecstatic reviews – just edgy enough to give you all a thrill but safe enough not to scare the horses – 'We are the One True Church! Keepers of the Flame'

Irina Where's this come from? If you could / hear yourself!

Konstantin But every once in a while a heretic like me comes along and exposes the rotten foundations and threatens to bring the whole sorry edifice crashing down around you –

Irina (*cod-German*) Oh, my son ze Decadent!

Konstantin And while you're at it, you can fuck off back to Mother Theatre and act in another one of your tawdry, predictable, mediocre little diversions, you sour-faced old mare

Irina I have *never* been mediocre. Who do you think you're talking to, you jumped-up son of a Kiev salesman, I mean who do you think you are? You couldn't even open a play in your own back garden – literally! You just feed off me, don't you, sucking the life from me, like a parasite

Konstantin At least I'm not a laughing stock

Irina No, darling, 'cause that would mean someone had noticed you

Oh God, please don't. Please don't. Oh darling, I am the worst mother who ever walked the earth. My baby, you must forgive me, you must, I don't mean these things. We've got to stick together, you're all I've got

Konstantin She doesn't love me any more. I've lost everything. I can't write. There's no point

Irina I know, I know, I know, we'll get through this, we will, you and me, we always do. I'm taking him away. She'll love you again, she will, I promise

See. No need for tears. Friends?

Konstantin nods.

Please, darling. For my sake, be civil to him, I'm not asking much – for me? And all this duel business – yes?

Konstantin Okay. Okay!

Enter Boris.

I can't talk to him though, Mummy

Irina All right all right all right

Konstantin It's too much right now

Konstantin notices Boris.

The good doctor will see to my bandage when he turns up

Boris One-two-one, eleven and twelve. 'If ever you find yourself short of a life, take mine'

Exit Konstantin.

Irina Right, well, the horses should be ready by now, so –

Boris 'If ever you find yourself short of a life, take mine'

Irina Sounds like something one of your characters would say

Boris It is something one of my characters says

Why do I find this simple plaintive appeal so moving?

Irina I expect it's because you wrote it – you're packed, I take it?

Boris One more day!

Irina Now listen to me, I know why you want to stay but let's not make fools of ourselves. You've spent too much time drinking beer by that lake and now you're a little woozy on the fumes, you need to sober up

Boris *You* need to sober up. Okay, we're both rational people here. If you were my friend – no, listen – you are capable of such generosity, I am asking you to be a true friend

Irina You're asking me to let you fuck her

Boris It's like there's a voice calling me – this could be just what I need

Irina The cold dead kiss of a child?

Boris My writing!

Irina Oh, how little you know yourself

Boris I am sleepwalking through life. You're talking to me, you're standing there, but all I see and hear is her. I'm possessed by such sweet visions of her soul – set me free

Irina I can't hear this, I won't, it's not happening

Boris It's in your power to release me from this torment

Irina You can't talk to me like this, I'm just a woman like any other –

Boris You're not a woman like any other, you're extraordinary, I'm giving you the chance to show how extraordinary you really are

Irina Boris, you're scaring me

Boris You're better than this – we both are – don't be so small, these *values*, what are they? Let's show them what true love is! I need to feel. I never did this. I read books, I didn't go to drama school. Look, it's not, it's nothing, it's just sexual, it's – no, okay, it's more than that, I'm an honest man and I won't lie to you, I can't – this is love, real love. The love of the poets and history and it takes one out of oneself into a realm of dreams far beyond and above mere flesh, she is the key to all my happiness

Irina Are you out of your tiny mind?

Boris This is so bourgeois – you and I, we're different!

Irina God, these *men*!

Boris She refuses to understand, why won't she understand?

Irina Am I really so old and ugly you can talk about other women to my face?

Boris Please! I beg you

Irina Oh my dear man

I see it all so clearly

Boris What what what does that mean?

Irina My poor sweet man

Boris What's that, what's that look?

Irina You've lost your senses, haven't you?

My beautiful man, I'm here now, I'm here, Irina's here

Boris What are you –

Irina You complete me

Boris I com— No, don't do that

Irina Don't do what?

Boris Whatever it is you're doing

Irina My joy, my pride, my bliss. If you left me for one hour, I'd go quite mad, I would die

Amazing magnificent man, lord of my soul, master of my desire, without you I'm nothing, a mere woman

Boris Someone might come in

Irina Let them. I'm not ashamed of my love for you, my treasure, my heart's –

Boris Stay back

Irina You're a man, oh God how I see you're a man, you want to do mad things, of course you do, but you're not like other men, I won't let you, I don't want you to, you mustn't, you can't. These eyes are mine. This hair, this forehead, these ears, mine, all mine. So talented, so clever, the best of men, every inch the writer! Your country needs you, glorious creature, Russia's last hope!

So simple, honest, true, fresh, funny and strong, with each stroke of your pen you convey the universe within a man's eyes and a woman's heart! No one writes women like you –

Boris Don't they?

Irina Brimming with life, passion, such heights of ecstasy, you think I exaggerate? Look into my eyes, oh to experience the full extent of your genius, my darling, I am your fulfilment, the one who makes you who you need to be. I alone can save you. I alone speak the truth. You're coming, aren't you? Stay with me, stay with me!

Boris I can't! I never know what I want

Irina You can, I see it, I see it in your eyes

Boris I've no mind of my own, no backbone – I'm still that fat little boy from school, oh God I'm such a shit!

Irina Got him

Irina gathers herself, lights a cigarette. Looks for an earring dropped during the tussle.

Look, I'm heading off, but if you fancy staying on a few days, don't let me get in your way –

Boris No, no, I'll come

Irina Sure? Spot of fishing, join me in civilisation in a week or so? No? Up to you

What are you writing?

Boris Turn of phrase I heard earlier – 'virgin country'. Might pinch it for a thing

Enter Ilya.

So, on the road again! Scything through the countryside, first class. Conversations in compartments! Trains eh?

Ilya The horses are ready. Train leaves a little after two. It's that time

Irina is still looking for her earring.

While you're in Moscow, ask after a certain actor for me – Suzdaltsev. We were old drinking buddies. He once told me this story about a time he was in a play with the great Ismailov. No rush, madam, you'll be glad you stayed for this

So one night Suzdaltsev realised he'd left his tobacco in the rehearsal room and he pops back in. Everyone was in the pub – or so he thought – because as he pushes the door open, who does he see but Ismailov, standing upright, behind one of the younger members of the cast – bent double over a prop samovar. In flagrante

Ilya picks Irina's earring up from the floor.

My mate Suzdaltsev doesn't know what to say – what do you say? Ismailov, this legendary figure, is giving this younger fella a fair old crack of the whip. So he just stands there, my mate, open-mouthed. And after a few moments – you'll love this – Ismailov, cool as anything, he says, 'Do you mind, old boy? We're just going over one of the scenes.'

At which point, my mate Suzdaltsev says, quick as a flash, 'I think that young fella might be having some trouble with his lines. I saw him going over the exact same scene last night with the director. The exact same scene'

This what you're after?

Ilya hands Irina her earring.
   Enter Yakov, who removes the last of the luggage.
Enter Polina.

Polina I picked these this morning and thought of you. Thought you'd like some fresh plums to nibble on for the journey

Irina You're very kind, Polina

Polina Goodbye, my lady! And if anything wasn't as it should be –

Irina Oh nonsense, I'd be lost without you. Now come on, don't start crying or you'll set me off too

Polina We've so little time left

Irina It's so true, so true. Darling, you might need to let go of my hand

Enter Semyon, with a spring in his step, and Petr.

Petr Sweetheart, you're going to miss your train

Semyon I'm going to run to the station, see you off! I'll meet you down there

Enter Yakov.
   Exit Semyon.

Irina For your exertions

Irina tips Yakov.

Petr I'll be in the carriage

Irina Farewell dear friends. Until next summer. Assuming we're not all dead – which at this rate is a distinct possibility

Ilya Don't forget to write! And don't be a stranger, Boris

Irina Where's my son? Will someone tell him I'm off, I can't not say goodbye

Exit all except Yakov, who is alone on stage.
Boris has left a packet of cigarettes. Yakov lights and smokes one.
Enter Boris.

Left my fags

Enter Nina.
Exit Yakov. He keeps the cigarettes.

Boris We're off

Nina I'm leaving tomorrow, leaving behind my father, my stepmother, the lake, all this, everything I've ever known. Boris Trigorin, I'm coming to Moscow. I'm going to act

Boris scribbles Nina a note.

Boris Hotel Slavyansky. Give them this. They know me there.

Nina Wait –

Boris I have to go. You're so lovely. Untouched, oh God!

I'm bewitched

Four

Manuscripts and notebooks.
  A bin.
  Enter Masha and Semyon.
  Yakov is on watch – he does the rounds, appearing
sporadically.

Masha Konstantin! Konstantin!

No one

Old man keeps asking, 'Where's Kostya? Where's Kostya?'

Semyon He's scared of dying alone

Masha There's waves on the lake

Semyon Been like this two days

Masha Waves!

Semyon Pitch black out there. Wind how it is, should've told Yakov to tear down what's left of Konstantin's stage – comes loose, could blow across the lawn straight through those windows. Just rotting anyhow. There's a piece of timber, the wind howls when it passes through – last night, as I passed, I could've sworn I heard a woman crying

Masha And so it goes

Semyon Masha, let's go home

Masha I'm staying

Semyon Our baby

Masha Your sister can feed him

Semyon He needs his mother. It's been three nights now

Masha At least you used to bore me with your theories about horseflies. Now it's all 'Masha come home, Masha the baby'

Semyon We're going

Your father won't give me a horse

Masha Have you even asked?

Enter Polina with bed linen, sets about making up a temporary bed.

Semyon Tomorrow, will you come home then?

Masha Yes! Stop going on about it

Masha lights a cigarette.
Enter Konstantin.

Polina He wants a bed in here with Konstantin

Masha I'll do it

Masha takes over the making of the bed.

Polina Children and old men

Polina peers at the manuscript.

Semyon I'll be off then

Bye, Masha

Semyon leans in to kiss Masha, who moves away.
Semyon tries to kiss Polina.

Mother

Polina I told you not to call me that

Polina flinches away.

If there's a God I'm sure he loves you

Semyon Konstantin

Exit Semyon.

Polina Who'd have thought? Little Kostya. Getting paid
to write

So handsome

All it takes is a little kindness. She's a good girl. She
won't cause you any bother

Masha Leave him alone

Polina I understand these things

Exit Konstantin.

Masha Perfect. Thanks

Polina I'm trying to help

Masha Don't

Polina I have eyes. I'm not blind

Masha Such a fuss. All this love and despair, it's like a
bad novel. Bollocks to it all. Tired of waiting for the
weather to change. Love's like the rain, it finds a way in.
They've promised my darling husband a job in another
district. Sooner we're gone the better. Out of sight, as
they say

A piano, off.

Polina He only plays when he's in one of his moods

Masha dances with quiet dignity.

Masha Wish they'd hurry up with that bloody transfer.
New beginnings. 'S all bollocks, all of it

*Enter Yevgeny and Semyon, pushing Petr in his
wheelchair.*

Semyon Six of us now, in the same room. Price of bread's gone up too

Yevgeny We all have our crosses to bear

Semyon You're all right, you haven't got mouths to feed

Yevgeny I am not all right, thank you very much. Eighty hours a week for thirty years, evenings, weekends – what do I have to show for it? A few grand and I've just blown that travelling

Masha You still here?

Semyon They won't give me a horse

Masha Should've died the day I met you

Yevgeny Well, I like what you've done with it. What have you done, turned it into a study?

Masha It's for Konstantin. A writer needs a room to work. Looks out over the lake and he can go out to the garden if he needs somewhere to think

Yakov comes through, wet. Enters and exits.

Petr Where's my sister?

Yevgeny Being picked up from the station with Boris, she'll be back soon

Petr If the pair of them have been summoned, I must be in a bad way

Still won't give me anything you know

Yevgeny What do you fancy? Whisky and a tub of aspirin? Cheeky shot of morphine, take the edge off?

Petr Ha bloody ha. Worst part about being stuck in this thing, can't get away from this old quack – that for me?

Polina All for you

Petr Thank you

Yevgeny half hums/half sings a line from 'Jolene' by Dolly Parton – about her eyes and skin.

Petr Kostya, here's one. It's about regret. It's called 'The Man Who Wanted It'. Or *L'homme qui a voulu* as I like to think of it. Once upon a time there was a young man who wanted to be a man of letters, you know the sort who holds forth about life and so on. But he never managed it. Every time he opened his mouth all that came out was the most frightful blather and no one paid him the slightest bit of attention – '*Mange tout*, dear boy, *mange tout*' and so on. Even when he had to do his summing up in court the jury would fall asleep. He wanted to experience all life had to offer but he never did. He wanted to go to Istanbul, but he never did –

Yevgeny For God's sake

Petr He wanted to live in a town. He wanted a wife

Yevgeny He wanted to become a state councillor, and guess what, he did

Petr *Acting* state councillor, and he didn't want it, it just happened. One day he was a promising young lawyer handing in an application, now here he is, seeing out his days in a wheelchair in the country

Yevgeny Oh, the chap in the story's you?

Petr Yes he is

Yevgeny Little undignified don't you think, moaning about life at your age?

Petr Dammit, I want to live! Why's that so hard to understand?

Yevgeny We all die sooner or later. That's how the story goes

Petr Look at you, back from living it up on your grand tour, the cat who's had all the bloody cream. Well, I haven't had any cream! I'm telling you, one day you're going to look death in the eye and I promise you, you won't be smiling then

Yevgeny The fear of death is an irrational fear. You've got to stamp it down. Only people who have cause to fear death are those who believe in an afterlife where your sins are punished. Now – you don't believe in an afterlife, and even if you did, you haven't done any sinning. All you've got to show for yourself is twenty-five years – (*starts to laugh*) sat on your arse in the town hall!

Petr Twenty-eight years, thank you

Enter Konstantin. He settles near Sorin.

Yevgeny We're in your way

Konstantin It's fine

Semyon Doctor, may I ask what your favourite city was, on your travels?

Yevgeny Genoa

Konstantin Why Genoa?

Yevgeny You walk out your hotel of an evening into a sea of bodies, swept along in the crowd – swirling and eddying, there's an energy, a confluence – joy, serenity, laughter, sex, the whole shebang – you're part of it, and it's part of you, this living organism. Strange sense of communion, as if there really is some universal human consciousness – like the one Nina spoke of in your play. How's she doing?

Konstantin I don't know, I've not seen her

Yevgeny I heard she'd taken a wrong turn. Know anything about that?

Konstantin It's quite a long story

Yevgeny Make it short. You're the writer

Konstantin She ran away to Moscow where Boris Trigorin fucked her night and day in a room he borrowed from his publisher. Short enough for you?

He got her pregnant and got bored I suppose and so he rekindled some old flames, shall we say? I say old, he never really ends relationships. Not the sort. I suppose Nina didn't really fit in with his plans. Oh, and along the way, the child died, I don't know the details

Yevgeny Is she acting?

Konstantin She's even less suited to the stage than she is to life, if you can imagine that. Started in some of the smaller theatres in Moscow. Understudied Ophelia. Saw everything she did for a while, followed her on tour. She got good roles. Well, lots of lines, anyway. But her acting was all a bit last-century. Clenched jaw and gestures. Emoting. There were flashes of something but usually only when she was dying or screaming or both. Just flashes though

Yevgeny So she could act?

Konstantin It was hard to tell to be honest, under all the hoopla, but yes, I suppose. Tried to see her actually, hung around stage doors and her digs, but she wasn't interested. Told people not to –

What else you want to know? Soon as she knew I'd gone she started writing to me. Acerbic, beguiling letters. Maybe she was the writer. She put a brave face on it but you could tell she was unhappy. The writing had a fraught quality actually, more I think about it, some of the letters were really weird, full of bizarre images. Signed herself 'Seagull'

She's back

Yevgeny Back? What, here?

Konstantin Room above a pub, in town, the other end. Been there five days. I was going to pop by, but Masha says she doesn't want visitors. (*To Semyon.*) You said you saw her yesterday evening, didn't you, out in the fields?

Semyon She was heading the other way. I said she should stop by. She said she would

Konstantin She won't

Her father and stepmother disowned her. They've got dogs patrolling, they won't let her within a mile of the house

It's easy being wise on paper, isn't it, Doctor? Bit harder in the real world

Petr She wore a white dress

Yevgeny Sorry?

Petr I said she wore a white dress. In the sunlight. The acting state councillor had rather a thing for her at one time

Yevgeny You old dog

Laughter, off.

Polina They're back

Konstantin I can hear Mummy

Enter Ilya, Irina and Trigorin.

Ilya Time makes fools of us all – buffeted by the winds of progress – except you, dear lady, the same young woman who played Juliet all those years ago

Irina Oh you awful man, I never get bored of you

Boris Petr! Not still poorly are you, that's no good
Masha! How the devil are you?

Masha Surprised you recognised me

Boris Married?

Masha Oh yes

Boris Happy?

*Boris acknowledges Yevgeny and Semyon. Only
Konstantin is left to greet.*

Your mother tells me you ah . . .

. . .

Konstantin shakes Boris' hand.

Irina Boris brought a magazine with your new story. It's
in there with one of his

Boris Yes, I –

*Boris hands Konstantin the magazine.
Polina and Ilya set up a card table.*

Konstantin Thank you

Boris Your admirers send their greetings. That pen name
of yours has them all a-tizz. Who is The Man Behind The
Mask? Or Woman. For some reason, a lot of them think
you're a woman

Konstantin Staying long?

Boris No, wish I could, I really do. Off back to Moscow,
early. This bloody anthology wants a story and someone
wants me to adapt a book for a thing, you know what it's
like, always on your case. This wind is biblical. If it drops
I'll pass by the lake first thing, see my friends the fish
before we off

I was going to stop by that . . . where your play was on, you remember? I'm working something up – not sure what it is yet, but I'm thinking about using that whole performance as a kind of backdrop to the main event, you don't mind do you?

Masha Father, Semyon needs a horse

Ilya A horse? Do we have any of those?

They've just been to the station and back, I can't send them out again when it's like this

Masha They're not the only horses

Semyon It's fine, Masha, I can walk

Masha (*to Ilya*) There's no point even talking to you, is there?

Polina You're going to walk in this weather?

Polina sits at the card table.

Okay, let's get started

Semyon Four miles isn't that far

Everyone makes preparations for cards.

I'll um. (*To Masha.*) I'll see you soon. (*To Polina.*) Polina

Semyon's prolonged exit causes suppressed hilarity.

I don't want to but –

I would stay it's just –

The baby –

I'll see myself out

Semyon finally goes. A chorus of laughter.

Ilya He'll be all right. Maybe he can catch a lift with a passing trawler

More laughter.

Polina While we're young

Ilya, Masha, Yevgeny, Polina, Irina and Boris play cards. Konstantin stands or sits apart.

Irina (*to Boris*) When the autumn evenings start drawing in, we all play Lotto – it's like, oh you'll pick it up. We've had this set since we were wee 'uns, it belonged to our mother. Come on, have a round before supper, you can see how us country folk keep ourselves amused

It's mortifying really but it's actually not bad once you get in the swing

Irina deals three cards to everyone.

Konstantin My story's not even in this one. Just an advert for it being in next month's. His is

Irina Kostya darling, I'm dealing, you in or out?

Konstantin I'm out

Exit Konstantin.

Irina Ten each to stay in, I might have to ask the good doctor to sub me

Yevgeny *Bien sûr*

Masha Any more? All right, twenty-two

Irina Yes!

Masha Three

Yevgeny Uh-huh

Masha Did you put it –

Seven. Eighty-one. Ten

Ilya Stop rushing, girl

Irina I haven't told you about Kharkov, goodness, my head's spinning just thinking about it

Masha Thirty-four

Irina It was the coming-out parade or whatever it's called

Yevgeny Coming-out parade?

Irina Oh you know, for the students, graduation, that's what I mean and I was handing out –

Masha Forty-two

Irina I was handing out their degrees and they gave me three bouquets, a standing ovation and this

Irina unfastens a brooch and tosses it on to the table.

Ilya Very nice

Irina I was very touched, I even gave a little speech

Masha Twelve

Yevgeny I'm sure you did

Irina They'd worked so hard

Masha Fifty

Yevgeny Five-O?

Irina Anyway, I looked marvellous. Say whatever you like, I've always known how to make an entrance

A piano, off.

Polina Konstantin. He's not been well

Ilya Papers went for his last one

Masha Seventy-seven

Irina As if anyone pays any mind to reviews

Boris He's so nearly there. There's just too many ideas vying. Can't find his voice, the writing has a self-conscious spectral quality like he's half in the shadows

Masha Four

Boris There's times it's almost feverish. And his stories seem populated almost entirely by ghosts

Masha Eleven

Irina (*to Petr*) We keeping you up?

Yevgeny The acting state councillor is no longer with us

Nodded off

Irina God, don't do that

Masha Seven. Ninety

Boris If I lived next to a lake, I'd never get any work done, I'd fish all day

    Enter Konstantin, unnoticed.

Masha Twenty-eight

Boris Catching a perch or a bream, the moment it takes, now that's true happiness

Yevgeny Well, I believe in Konstantin! I think he's got something. He thinks in images, I find them unsettling in a good way, they're haunting, and that's not such a bad thing, is it? All right, I'm missing a sense of what he's trying to do. His stories have an effect, I'm just not sure what's underneath. Irina, are you pleased your son's a writer?

Irina Would you believe, I haven't read a thing he's written – I would, but there's always so much on

Masha is the first to notice Konstantin. When she fails to call the number, the others look at her – then they notice him.

Masha Twenty-six

Ilya Boris, we've still got something of yours

Boris Sorry, what?

Ilya Konstantin once shot a bird. An arctic tern

Masha Sixty-six

Ilya You wanted it mounted

Konstantin Can't believe how dark it is. Strangest sensation

Irina Do shut that, darling, there's a draught

Masha All the eights

Boris And, ladies and gentlemen, that is your lotto

Irina Oh you swine, bravo!

Ilya Indeed

Irina Can't seem to leave the house without getting lucky these days

Right, our celebrity guest has yet to eat. We can have more games after supper. Darling, leave that

Konstantin I'm not hungry, Mummy

Irina Up to you

She wakes Petr.

Petr darling. Supper time

Irina takes Ilya by the arm.

Now. Kharkov. I'll tell you all about it

*Exit all. Polina and Yevgeny push Petr in his wheelchair.
Konstantin is alone.*

Konstantin I hear it's the first sign of madness, talking to yourself. Keep thinking I hear her but it's all in my head

I've rather painted myself into a corner – in my writing, I mean. Spend so much energy trying to avoid the old traps, just seem to fall into new ones

Boris has his tricks. His characters are all curiously observant and articulate, forever noticing telling details, like writers funnily enough. And if at any point you find anything mysterious or ambiguous, don't panic, sooner or later there'll be a speech where everything is explained. And I mean everything. At length. While the other characters sort of stand back and let whoever's doing the explaining get on with it

Seems to praise every other writer but me

He's actually rather good. It works, and when all's said and done, that's the thing. I used to want to change the world. Now I'd be happy just to tell a simple story well and with conviction

I over-egg things, you see, with me, a thing's never a thing, it always represents something. I keep giving characters names like Grace and Hope – I know, shoot me

Art is more than spectacle. You can't put it in a box. You have to write what's inside you, even if everyone says you're wrong, even if –

Hello?

Enter Nina.

Is it really you?

I've replayed this moment endlessly, back and forth. Please don't cry. Let me touch you

Nina Someone's watching

Konstantin No one's here, it's just us

Nina Lock the doors, no one must see

Konstantin No one will come in

Nina Your mother's here, I've seen her

Konstantin Okay, okay –

I'll put a chair here. Don't be scared, we won't be disturbed

Nina Let me look at you

It's nice in here. Almost feel my fingers again. This was the sitting room

Why are you looking at me like that?

Konstantin You've lost weight. Your eyes are bigger

Nina All the better to see you with

Konstantin You've been here nearly a week, I thought you'd never come. I've been to your digs morning, noon and night, looking up at your window – someone threw me a coin

Nina I thought you hated me. Every night, in my dream, I call out to you and you look straight through me. I've been out by the lake, wandering. I never know how but I always seem to end up here. Waiting to be invited in. Like one of your vampires

Shall we have some tea? No, let's talk. So warm. Hear that? The wind. I'll do you some Turgenev. 'A good thing it is for' – no. 'A good thing it is for a man who, on such nights, sits under his own roof, in a warm corner like a seagull.' Hang on. Where was I? 'And may God protect the wanderer with nowhere to rest her head.' I'm not sure I got that right. Oh what difference does it make?

Konstantin Nina, Nina, Nina

Nina So yesterday evening, I went to see if our little theatre was still there, and I burst into tears for the first time in two years – honestly, God, sometimes all you need is a good cry – did I already say that? It's all right, I've stopped now

You're a writer, I'm an actress, oh there's no end to it. I used to dream of fame. I used to wake up singing, with sheer joy, like a child and I loved you and tomorrow I'm off to Yelets –

Konstantin What did you say?

Nina I'm off to Yelets, first thing –

Konstantin Did you –

Nina Wonderful Yelets, come to Yelets, where the fuck is Yelets? I hope I get a seat. I do well in Yelets. Never have to buy my own drinks if you know what I mean. Life is – it's like sandpaper

Konstantin Why Yelets?

Nina What kind of question's that? I'm doing the winter season, it's a job, course I've got to go

Konstantin I cursed you, Nina. I loathed you. Your letters and photographs I tore up and I burned, every last one but I knew – knew – that my soul is bound to yours until the end of time. I tried to stop loving you. I can't. Don't have the strength. After you left I heard I was going to be published and I knew this was the universe speaking – this was divine justice, God answering me across the cosmos. I was wrong. My life has been –

I feel two hundred thousand years old. But now. I've been calling you, Nina – there's a cord binding us together. I worship the ground beneath your feet, I kiss it. I see your face in all nature. This tender sun that shone upon me in the best days I ever knew, and you're here, oh God, Nina, I love you –

Nina Why's he doing this, why does he have to talk like this?

Konstantin I've been so cold and lonely. No one can reach my heart. I've been buried in the depths of the earth for so long now and it's dry and there is no air or light, please, Nina, stay, stay, stay or I'll come with you! I'll come with you!

For God's sake! Why did you come?

Nina They're waiting for me at the gates. Please. Don't see me off. You can't

Can I have some water?

Konstantin pours her some water. She drinks it all down. He refills it.

Konstantin Where are you going?

Nina To find someone who'll buy me a drink

Is she here?

Konstantin Uncle Petr took a bit of downward turn so we sent for her

Nina Why did you have to say you kissed the ground I walked on?

You ought to kill me. I wish someone would

I'm so tired, if I could find a place to rest – rest! I am the seagull. I am the – no, that's not it, I never seem to get it –

I'm an actress, I can –

Irina and Boris laughing, off.

He's here too, isn't he? Of course he is. D'you know what, doesn't bother me any more? It really doesn't. You know he doesn't even like theatre? I mean, doesn't believe, not like us. He used to laugh at me, at my dreams and after a while I stopped believing too

And I got really petty, embarrassing stuff, could feel it happening. At first I was fine, you know, being at home with my little boy. I got jealous, which is silly really. Felt myself shrinking. Till eventually there was nothing left. It came across in the acting. My voice gave me away, I never knew what to do with my hands. Always stood in the wrong place

You'll never know what that's like. Up there in front of all those people and they're laughing at you and they're right

I am the seagull – no. No

Do you remember you shot a seagull? Idea for a story – a man comes along and for no reason at all he destroys it. You remember?

Konstantin Wrong one

Nina I mean it's not like that any more, now I'm a real actress, acting gives me pleasure, it's a joy, I feel beautiful and confident, when I'm on stage I feel intoxicated with the sheer wonder of it all. I'm alive, keep marching on, and every day I grow stronger inside

You see, this I do know, Konstantin. That in our work – it's not about fame or glory or money. It's about who can endure. We all have a cross to bear. And when I believe, when I truly believe – I don't feel the weight of that cross digging into my shoulder and in those moments – nothing scares me. Not even life

Konstantin I'm glad you found your path. I wish I'd found mine. There's chaos in my head I don't know what

89

it's for, what to do with it. I'm afraid I've lost faith. There's nothing left to believe in

Nina Don't say that. You mustn't. When I'm a great actress you'll come and watch me, won't you? Promise me you'll come and watch me. It's late. I can hardly stand. I'm shattered. I never eat

Konstantin I'll fetch you something, you can have –

Nina Please don't. Don't see me off. I'll go on my own. Can hear the dog barking

I love him

I love him more than I ever did

I love him till my bones splinter and crack

Don't say anything. When you see him

Subject for a short story

It was good once, wasn't it? You remember?

So bright. Full of joy. Laughter – so fragile

I howl into the void. And hear nothing back

All living creatures. Antelope and eagle. Hummingbird and lion. Mollusc and rat

Bone

Stone

Gone

None remains, except I –

I am Mars. I am Venus. I am Alexander. I am Joan

Man, Woman, Beast

The consciousness of every living thing

Exit Nina.

Konstantin I should tell Mummy Nina's here

Actually, probably not, wouldn't want to worry her

> *Konstantin stares at his manuscript.*
> *After an age he slowly tears a sheet in two. Then he rips it again, and continues, faster and faster until the whole thing is destroyed.*
> *Exit Konstantin.*
> *Enter Yevgeny.*

Yevgeny There's a chair

> *Enter Irina, Polina, Masha, Boris and Yakov, carrying wine and beer.*
> *Yakov pours himself a glass of water.*

Irina Red wine and, Boris, we got some beers in for you. We can drink and play

> *Yakov is about to drink his water, when:*

Polina Coffee and tea's probably not a bad idea either

> *Yakov exits.*
> *Ilya enters carrying a stuffed bird – a tern.*

Ilya This is what I was on about. You wanted it stuffed

Boris Did I?

Ilya It's an arctic tern – a sea bird

Boris Doesn't ring any bells

Arctic tern? Common tern, isn't it, what's an arctic tern doing this far inland?

> *A gunshot, off.*

Irina Now that sounded –

Yevgeny Balls, that's one of my bottles going off again in my bag, sorry, I'll –

Exit Yevgeny.
  Re-enter Yevgeny.

Yeah, bang goes another bottle of ether, sorry, they keep doing that

Dorn hums a short, familiar refrain from 'Some Enchanted Evening' by Rodgers and Hammerstein.

Irina Almost like that time when . . .

As Masha deals cards, Yevgeny takes Boris aside, shows him a magazine.

Yevgeny Boris, have you seen – reports from America of some terrible things going on in the name of – You need to get her out. That stupid boy, he's only gone and shot himself

Boris returns to the card game. He sits next to Irina.
  Yakov enters.
  Boris leans over to Irina and whispers.